Unusual Buildings

Debbie Croft

Contents

Buildings Around the World

There are some very unusual buildings throughout the world. Many of these buildings have been built in the last 100 years, and some are still in the planning stages. Mostly, it is the **exterior** designs that are different. Inside, many of these buildings have rooms, shops or offices that look the same as other ordinary buildings.

A large number of these unique buildings are designed by **architects** who specialise in creating **original** styles, and will draw attention to the finished buildings. Sometimes, the owner of a building wants to highlight a particular way of life. Some buildings represent a product that a company is trying to sell. On other occasions, the design of a building simply makes people want to visit it, to view its special features and to learn something about the person who created it.

The National Centre for the Performing Arts in Beijing, China, is also known as "The Giant Egg".

The Forest Spiral in Darmstadt, Germany, is an apartment building.

The Sydney Opera House   Sydney, Australia

The Sydney Opera House is a centre for performing arts. It is home to the Australian Opera, the Australian Ballet, the Sydney Theatre Company and the Sydney Symphony Orchestra.

An international design competition was held in 1956, to choose who would design this **iconic** building. More than 200 entries were received from architects around the world. Danish architect Jørn Utzon won first prize and 5000 pounds for his entry. Construction of the Sydney Opera House began in 1959.

The building is constructed on 588 concrete piers that have been sunk up to 25 metres below sea level. A series of "shells" form the roof, giving the building its **distinctive** design. These shells are covered in tiles, some of which are glossy white and others which are cream in colour. The main foyer has huge glass panels and the outer walls are covered in sections made of pink **granite**.

The Sydney Opera House is a major tourist attraction.

Since the Sydney Opera House was completed in 1973, it has become known as one of the twentieth century's most original buildings. It is famous throughout the world as a centre for performing arts. In 2007, the building was listed as a World Heritage Site.

Each year, over a million people visit the Sydney Opera House to view concerts by world-class performers.

Other people take tours just to observe the concert halls and visit backstage areas that are usually reserved for performers and their support teams.

Every year on New Year's Eve, thousands of people come to the Sydney Opera House to view the stunning fireworks display.

Think and Talk About ...

The Sydney Opera House is located on the shores of Sydney Harbour.

The fireworks display next to the Sydney Opera House takes place every year.

Cubic Houses Rotterdam, the Netherlands

The Cubic Houses in the Netherlands were designed and built in the 1970s. There are 38 houses attached to each other, with a large "super cube" at each end.

Each cubic house sits at an angle on a pole. It has concrete floors and pillars with a wooden frame. The building is well-**insulated**, with double-glazed windows for extra protection against the weather.

Some of the Cubic Houses contain hostel rooms for tourists.

Inside, the three levels are connected by a narrow staircase. The lower level is a triangular area that is used as a living room. The middle level contains a sleeping area and a bathroom. The top level can be used as an extra bedroom or another living area, depending on the number of people living there. This top section of the house provides a great view as it has windows on all sides.

The area below the cube is used as a storage area, and also has a staircase that leads to the entrance.

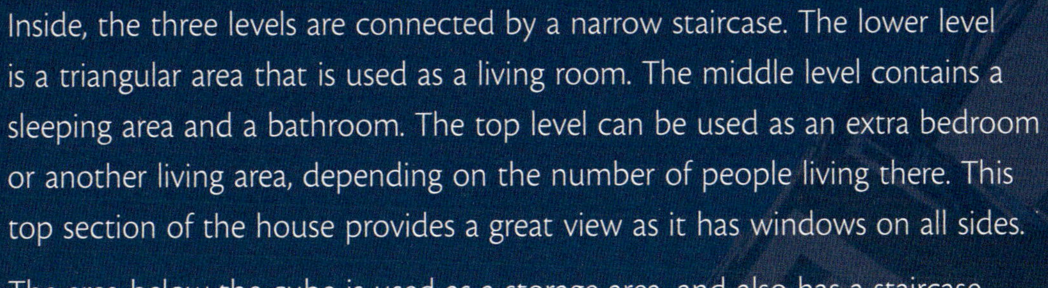

Think and Talk About ...

Each cubic house is described by the architects as a "tree", and collectively they represent a "forest".

The Lotus Temple New Delhi, India

New Delhi's Lotus Temple is a place of worship that is open to people of all religions. It has featured in hundreds of newspapers and magazine articles throughout the world since it was completed in 1986.
Its design imitates the magnificent lotus flower.

The Lotus Temple attracts tourists from around the world.

The temple has a nine-sided circular shape. It is made up of 27 "petals", arranged in three **concentric** circles. The outer circle has nine petals that face outwards, making a shelter over each of the entrances. The second ring covers the outer hall, and the inner ring partly encloses the centre of the building. The petals are made from concrete and are covered with white marble.

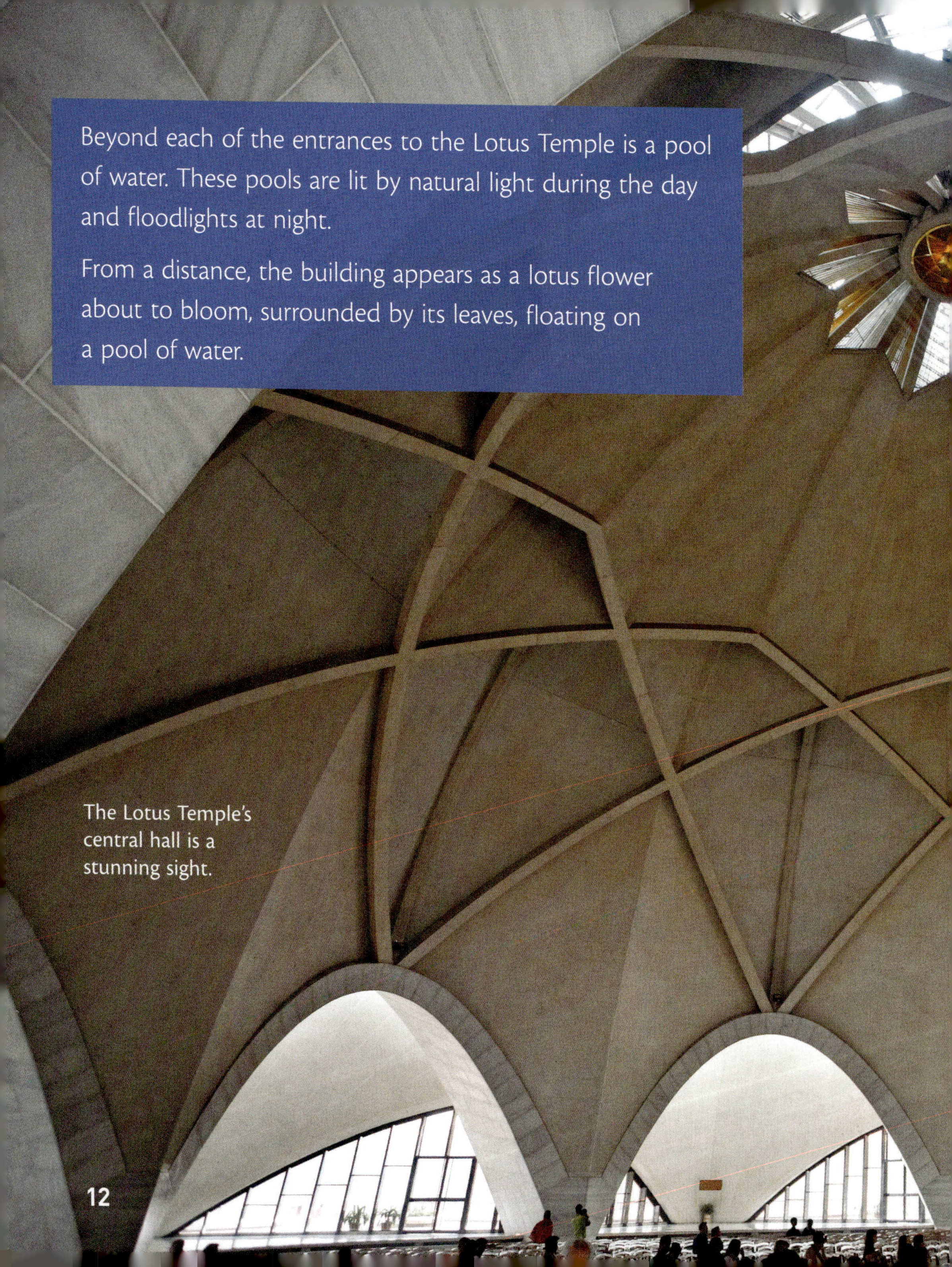

Beyond each of the entrances to the Lotus Temple is a pool of water. These pools are lit by natural light during the day and floodlights at night.

From a distance, the building appears as a lotus flower about to bloom, surrounded by its leaves, floating on a pool of water.

The Lotus Temple's central hall is a stunning sight.

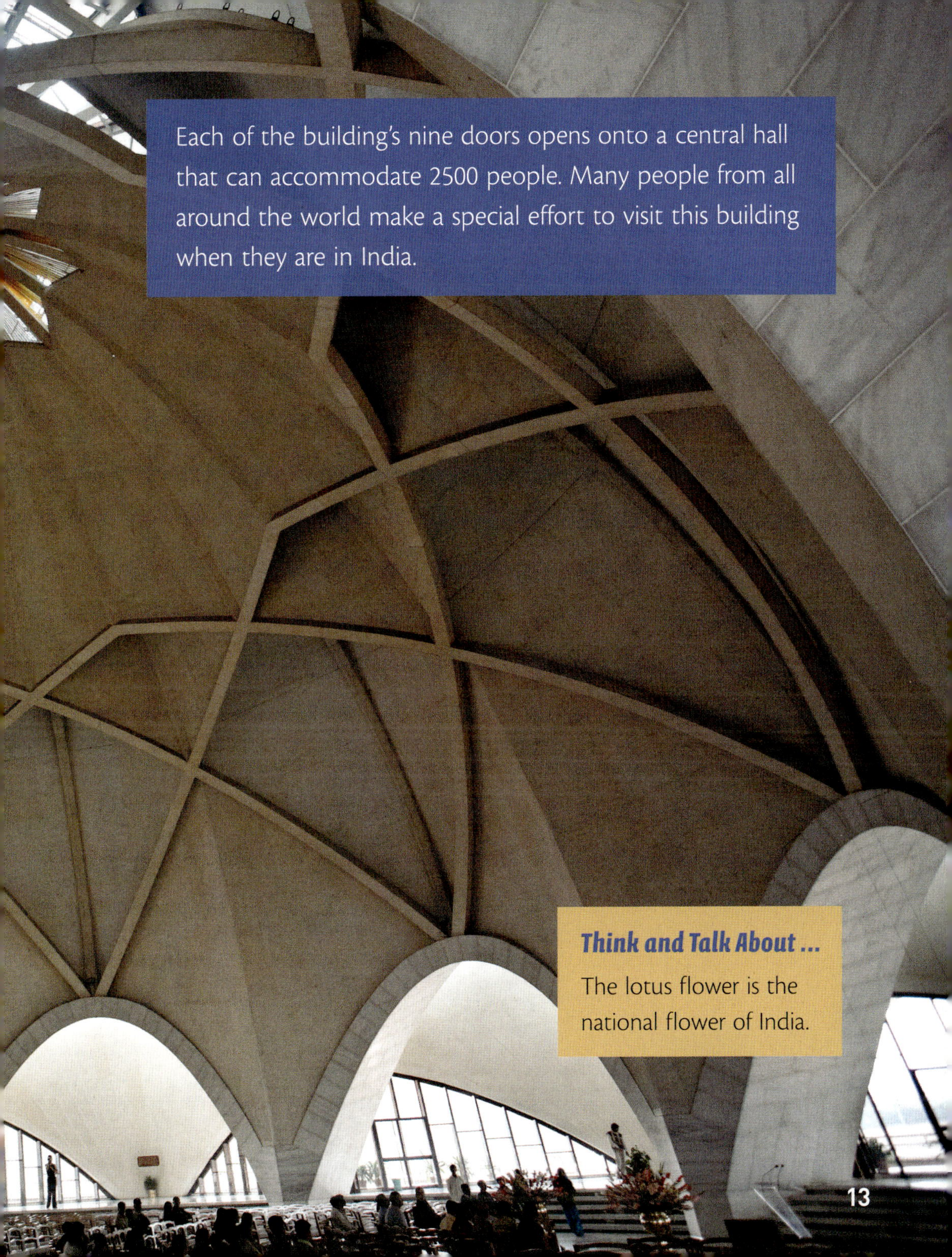

Each of the building's nine doors opens onto a central hall that can accommodate 2500 people. Many people from all around the world make a special effort to visit this building when they are in India.

Think and Talk About ...

The lotus flower is the national flower of India.

The Basket Building Ohio, the USA

The Basket Building is the headquarters of the Longaberger Company in Ohio, the USA.

This building, completed in 1997, is a replica of one of the company's woven shopping baskets that can be bought by customers all over the world. The **dimensions** of this building are 160 times larger than one of the original shopping baskets.

The two handles attached to the basket have also been included in the building design. During the cold winter months, these handles are continually heated, so there is no build-up of snow or ice to add extra weight to the top of the building.

The Basket Building has a steel structure that is covered with stucco, which is a mixture of cement, sand and lime. Stucco provides a strong and inexpensive surface that needs very little care after the building has been completed.

The inside of the building is spectacular, with a grand staircase and marble floors. The seven-storey building is topped with glass, so the handles of the basket can be seen from the inside.

The Longaberger Company's headquarters is unique.

Think and Talk About ...

The Basket Building is a clever form of advertising for the Longaberger Company.

The Crooked House Sopot, Poland

The Crooked House was constructed in the town of Sopot, Poland, in 2004. It forms part of a shopping centre that has restaurants, shops and a radio station. Its design is cartoon-like, based on the illustrations in a children's picture book.

There are colourful stained-glass entrances to the building, and the windows are framed by sandstone. The roof is covered with blue-green shingles resembling the scales on a dragon.

The building appears crooked because there are no right angles in its construction. The lines of the building are curved to create a moving and mysterious atmosphere.

The Crooked House is a popular tourist attraction in the city of Sopot. During the day, many people stop outside to take photographs before they wander through the building. At night-time, lights of different colours show off the building's unique features.

The design of the Crooked House is inspired by children's picture book illustrations.

www.krzywydomek.info

Kansas City Library *Missouri, the USA*

The Kansas City Library in Missouri, the USA, is a multi-storey complex. The first floor has a large open space that is used when guest speakers address visitors to the library. The second floor has a huge area specifically for children's books. The Grand Reading Room occupies the third and fourth floors. This room is lined with bookshelves containing thousands of books on many different topics. The fifth floor has a rooftop area that includes a life-sized chessboard.

The Grand Reading Room is on the third and fourth floors of the library.

Kirk Hall is found on the first floor of the library.

In 2006, a large parking area for the library was constructed to provide more car spaces in the busy downtown area of the city. Local residents were asked how they thought the area could be made more appealing. After a great amount of discussion, it was decided that the theme of the library would be extended to the car-park area. Therefore, a frontage that appears as a row of books on a bookshelf was constructed to disguise the car park. Members of the community were asked to **nominate** titles for the large "books" that would line the street near the library.

The unusual design of the car park attracts many visitors to the Kansas City Library.

The final list includes examples that represent a wide range of famous books written over many years. Each of the 22 book spines is 9 metres high and creates an **imposing** sight.

Some of the titles are:

- *The Adventures of Huckleberry Finn*
- *The Lord of the Rings*
- *Charlotte's Web*.

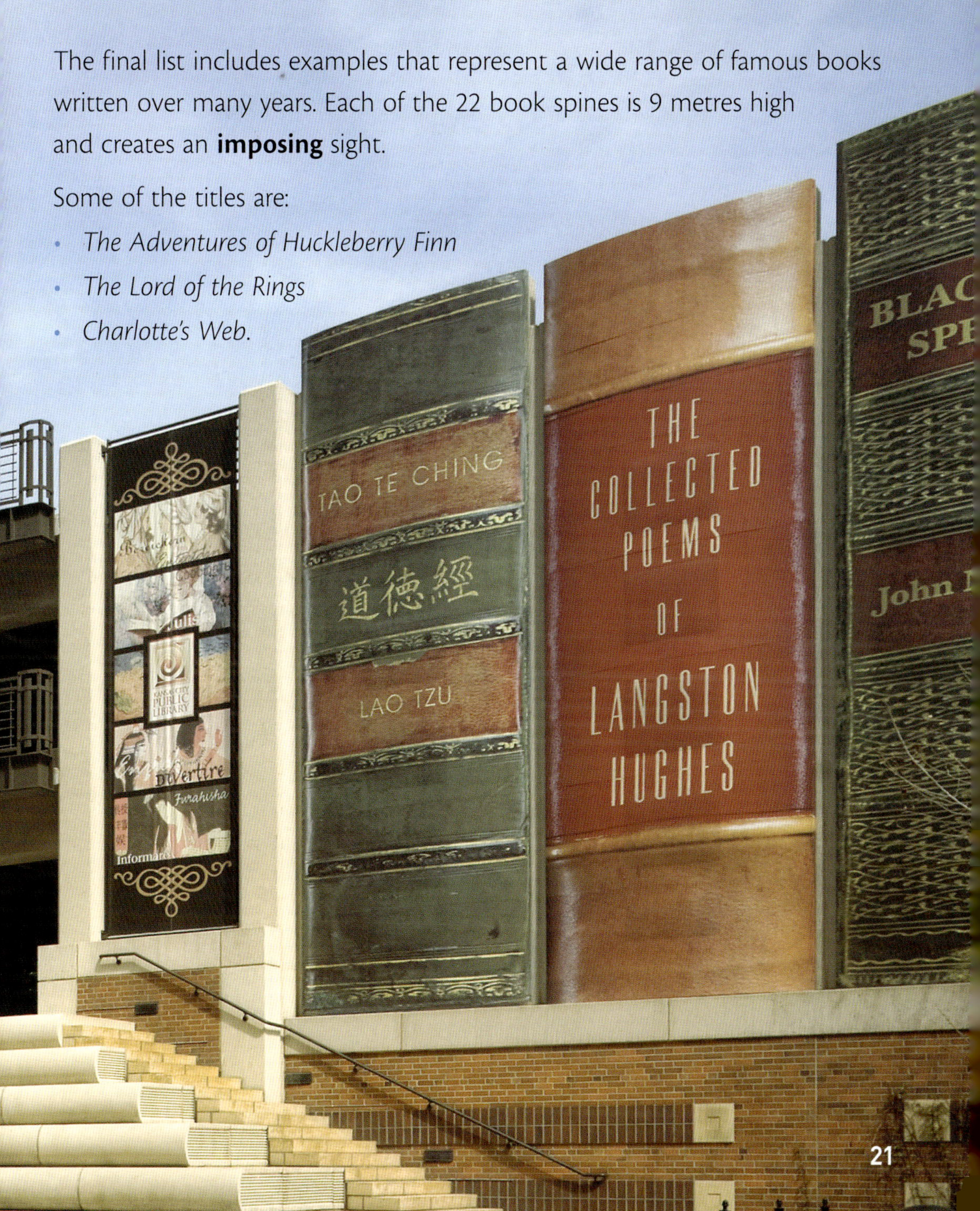

The Rotating Tower Dubai, United Arab Emirates

The Rotating Tower is a skyscraper proposed for the city of Dubai, in the United Arab Emirates. It will consist of **retail outlets**, a hotel, apartments and luxury villas. If the construction proceeds as planned, this building will feature some of the most technologically advanced concepts ever used in the building industry.

In an effort to reduce production costs and the number of workers needed, only the core of the building will be built at the construction site. **Modules** used to construct the tower will be put together in a factory and transported to the building site ready for installation. In this way, it is **anticipated** the building will be completed in less than two years.

The most unique feature of this building is that each of the 80 storeys will be able to rotate independently. This means that the building will have an almost unlimited number of shapes.

The entire building will be powered by **wind turbines** and solar panels. It is expected that the tower will create enough electricity to supply up to five additional buildings nearby.

Think and Talk About ...

It is considerably safer for people to work in a factory than on a high-rise construction site.

Creating Original Buildings

The construction of large and unusual buildings around the world is a complicated and time-consuming task. These projects require a considerable amount of funding and take years to construct. Large workforces in many different branches of the construction industry are often required to complete a single project.

Generally, the more original a building, the more thought has to go into the planning. It can take years for a building to come into existence, as many hours are involved in developing the concept and planning the design. Architectural drawings need to be produced. These large buildings also require accurate calculations about how they will be built and how much money they will cost.

Today, people marvel at how original some of the world's most unusual buildings are. They are generally more willing to appreciate original designs, as architects attempt to develop plans and concepts that challenge people's thinking and expectations.

Think and Talk About ...

As well as drawing sketches, architects create physical and digital models of buildings.

An architect works on a design.

The Woodland House

A unique woodland house was constructed as a private home for a family in Wales, in the United Kingdom. The house, which was designed by architect Simon Dale, was built in 2008.

The owner of the woods gave Simon and his family a section of land for free, after they offered to take care of the nearby woodland area. The family wanted to build a house that supported a natural, healthy lifestyle, so an **eco-friendly** home that blended with its surroundings was an ideal option for them. They wanted to create a sustainable lifestyle that had little impact on the environment.

The woodland house was built by the family, with some help from visiting friends and curious people passing by. The entire house, from start to finish, took just four months to complete.

The site for the house was chosen so it could be nestled into the hillside and be well protected from the weather. When the site was dug out, stone and mud was able to be reused for the foundations and retaining walls.

The timber frame was constructed first. It is made from spare wood recycled from the surrounding woodland.

Later, the roof was added. It is designed as a simple, self-supporting structure, and is also built using natural pieces of timber. It was quick to erect, but is extremely strong. The inside of the roof is lined with plastic sheets, to prevent moisture spoiling the interior of the house.

On the outside, the roof is covered with mud and grass. This **obscures** much of the house, which was a deliberate attempt by the owner to reduce the visual impact on the environment.

The floor, walls and roof of the house are lined with bales of straw. This is a very effective technique for insulating the house, particularly against the cold temperatures of the Welsh winter.

The exterior of the house resembles the hobbit houses in *The Lord of the Rings* movies.

Lime plaster has been used on the interior walls. This product can be manufactured using less energy compared to cement, so it was a sensible option to use in this part of the house. Recycled wood has been used for the floors and some of the other fittings included in the house. Many items, such as the windows, a wood burner, pipes for plumbing, and wiring were located in rubbish piles and adapted so they could be reused. Fuel for the wood burner is available in the nearby woodland area and is recognised as a renewable resource.

Air coming from underground and through the foundations cools the refrigerator. As in all modern homes, the refrigerator is used to store food at a temperature that is safe for people to eat.

During the daytime, a skylight in the roof allows the Sun's rays to provide natural lighting.

Solar panels produce energy for lighting at night-time or when the weather is wet or cloudy. Family members can access various forms of technology using this power source. They can play music and use their computer in the same way as people living in cities throughout the world.

The water from a nearby spring flows downhill and is channelled to the house for washing and cooking. Water that drains from the roof is collected in a pond and used to **cultivate** the garden. The family has learnt to reduce their water consumption, as the supply can only be replenished when good rain falls.

This house is equipped with a compost toilet, which does not rely on water to flush away waste. Over time, waste products are composted and can be reused to enrich the soil where vegetation grows.

Think and Talk About ...

In Wales, the sun sets at about 4 pm during winter.

The tools required to construct this house were as simple as the design itself. A chainsaw was used for cutting and shaping timber collected from the woods. A hammer and chisel were crucial for sculpting pieces of wood to fit the design, but very few other tools were needed.

The owner's **perseverance** played a major role in creating a comfortable and sustainable living space. He focused on the goal to produce an eco-friendly home that allowed his family and nature to exist together in harmony.

Simon Dale, the architect of the woodland house, completed much of the construction work himself.

Glossary

anticipated (*verb*)	expected and prepared for
architects (*noun*)	people who design buildings
concentric (*adjective*)	shapes that share the same centre
cultivate (*verb*)	to grow crops on land
dimensions (*noun*)	the measurements of a building or other object
distinctive (*adjective*)	when something has a special quality that makes it recognisable
eco-friendly (*adjective*)	good for the environment
exterior (*adjective*)	something that is on the outside
granite (*noun*)	a very hard rock used for building
iconic (*adjective*)	important and famous
imposing (*adjective*)	having an impressive appearance
insulated (*adjective*)	containing a layer to keep in warmth
modules (*noun*)	different parts of a building
nominate (*verb*)	to formally suggest something
obscures (*verb*)	covers up
original (*adjective*)	imaginative and clever
perseverance (*noun*)	carrying on and continuing with something
retail outlets (*noun*)	shops that sell various products
wind turbines (*noun*)	machines that use the power of the wind to produce electricity

Index